Angela

Mark Ravenhill

T0348075

methuen | drama

LONDON • NEW YORK • OXFORD • NEW DELHI • SYDNEY

METHUEN DRAMA
Bloomsbury Publishing Plc
50 Bedford Square, London, WC1B 3DP, UK
1385 Broadway, New York, NY 10018, USA
29 Earlsfort Terrace, Dublin 2, Ireland

BLOOMSBURY, METHUEN DRAMA and the Methuen
Drama logo are trademarks of Bloomsbury Publishing Plc

First published in Great Britain 2021

Cover design by Tjaša Krivec
Photography © Mark Ravenhill

A catalogue record for this book is available from the British Library.

ISBN: PB: 978-1-3502-5559-3
ePDF: 978-1-3502-5560-9
eBook: 978-13502-5561-6

Series: Play Anthologies, 1234567X, volume 4

Typeset by Mark Heslington Ltd, Scarborough, North Yorkshire

To find out more about our authors and books visit
www.bloomsbury.com and sign up for our newsletters.

Angela first premiered on 26 March 2021, in an audio production commissioned and produced by Sound Stage, with the following cast and creative team.

In alphabetical order

Julie, Nurse One and Plummy Woman	**Nadia Albina**
Doctor Adetiba (Doctor One) and Director	**Dermot Daly**
Older Angela	**Pam Ferris**
Doctor Mansoor (Doctor Two) and Plummy Man	**Raj Ghatak**
Younger Angela	**Matti Houghton**
Fox and Doctor Carter (Doctor Three)	**Olivier Huband**
Ted	**Toby Jones**
Young Mark	**Jackson Laing**
Angela's Mum, Ballet Teacher, Nurse Two and Ivy	**Alexandra Mathie**
Mark	**Joseph Millson**
Social Worker, Ballet Woman and Nurse Three	**Kirsty Stuart**

Writer   Mark Ravenhill
Director   Polly Thomas
Assistant Director   Emma Lynne Harley.
Composer   Alexandra Faye Braithwaite
Sound Recordist   Louis Blatherwick
Sound Design   John Scott

Angela is a Royal Lyceum Theatre Edinburgh and Pitlochry Festival Theatre production in association with Naked Productions Ltd and BBC Radio 3 for Sound Stage

Sound Stage commissions were made possible with support from Creative Scotland through its Performing Arts Venues Relief Fund

Royal Lyceum Theatre Edinburgh

The Royal Lyceum Theatre Edinburgh is one of the UK's most prolific theatre companies. Our beautiful, intimate Victorian theatre has played a significant role in the creative life of Edinburgh for over 130 years. The company draws upon the considerable talent in Scotland alongside partners across the globe, to make theatre in Edinburgh that can speak to the world. www.lyceum.org.uk

PITLOCHRY
Festival Theatre

Pitlochry Festival Theatre

Established 1951, Pitlochry Festival Theatre offers a unique theatrical experience, operating a daily repertoire system in the summer which means that audiences and visitors can enjoy six different productions in six days. We create, nurture and inspire, making theatre for everyone – theatre for a lifetime. www.pitlochryfestivaltheatre.com

Naked Productions Ltd

Naked Productions is a leading independent production company, making top quality, innovative audio for a range of platforms. www.nakedproductions.co.uk

An early draft of 'Angela' was given an online workshop reading by the Bristol University Players on June 20th 2020. Thanks to all those who took part: Lucy Gray, Anna Farthing, Marc Funda, Irena Grugulis, Michael de Bono, Loraine Adams, Tom Edward Phillips, Ian Gibson, Guy Undrill, Vincent Franklin, Brenda Kenworthy, Sheila Finlayson, Tanya Nash, Dave Barton, Italo Cadamuro, Bonnie Taylor, Tina Gwynne-Evans, Indie de Bono, Lily Dyble, Richard Ahsam, Louise Kavyasiddhi Mulvey, Karen Drury, Steve Taylor, Wendy Kenyon, Roger May, Rosanna Shearburn, John Pead, Pauline Pead, Sarah Benjamin, Kit Benjamin and Clare de Bono.

Angela

Characters

Angela
Mark
Ted
Julie
Mum
Little Girl
Fox
Director
Plummy Man
Plummy Woman
Ten-Year-Old Boy as Toad
Teacher
Older Woman
Woman
Policeman
Waiter
Ivy
Doctors
Nurses
Porter

One

Ballet music. At first, we hear it clean but then it cross-fades to come from a speaker in the corner of a ballet studio and plays throughout.

Teacher (*calling over the music*)   That's it, ladies, get into twos and I want you to travel – sorry ladies and gentlemen – gentleman – we're not used to having a man in the class are we, ladies? – but you're very welcome, Mark. Very welcome.

Chatter and laughter from 'the ladies'.

Into pairs, ladies and, and gentleman – and then I want you to travel – using the work that we – that's it. Very good. Excellent. And the next couple start travelling. Keep extending those arms. Wonderful turn-out, Sindu. And the next –

That's it, Mark. Don't worry about the feet. Just keep the arms – yes!

Incongruously a telephone rings.

Two

The music and the ballet class fade away until just a telephone is left ringing in a small suburban living room.

Angela (*aged eighty-four, internal*)   What's that noise?

Is it the baby?

Alright, darling. Mummy's coming.

(*Calls.*) Ted! Ted! It's the baby!

(*Internal.*) Where's Ted gone?

(*Calls.*) Ted!

(*Internal.*) She's still – There's a word for it – only I can't – telephone!

(*Calls.*) Ted! Telephone! Ted!

(*Internal.*) Has he run off? I'll show him. One day I'll run off. I'll put on a nice blouse and I'll go off and I'll – I'll – I'll go on a thing around the world.

What's the –?

Telephone. Alright. (*With great effort to push herself out of the chair.*) Mummy's coming.

She picks up the telephone. Her voice becomes instantly posher.

Angela 84   Hello?

Mark 52 (*on telephone, not too clear*)   Hello, Angela. How are you today?

Angela 84   Me? Not so bad. You know. Nice to see a bit of sunshine.

Mark 52   Would you like to go for a walk on Saturday?

Angela 84   Oh yes a walk on Saturday would be lovely.

Mark 52   I thought we could go through the woods on Saturday and then have a bit of cake.

Angela 84   Will it be walnut cake?

Mark 52   If they've got walnut cake yes you can have walnut cake.

Angela 84   Oooh, walnut cake that would be lovely. Excuse me please who am I speaking to?

Mark 52   You're speaking to Mark.

Angela 84   I see yes Mark. Mark.

Mark 52   I'm your son.

Angela 84   My son?

Mark 52   Your son. Who did you think I was?

Angela 84   I thought you were a handsome man come to take me away on a cruise.

Mark 52   I don't think Ted would like it if you went off with a handsome man on a cruise.

Angela 84   Oh Ted'd just have to lump it. A son? I remember a girl. Is there a girl?

Mark 52   A daughter?

Angela 84   Yes. My daughter. Could I speak to my daughter please?

Mark 52   There isn't a daughter, Mum.

Angela 84   Did they kill her like they killed my sister?

Mark 52   No you never had a daughter. Just a son.

Angela 84   Well, a son. That's good isn't it?

Ted 84 (*distant*)   Angie! Angie!

Angela 84   I gotta go. Ted's come back. (*Internal.*) I've got a baby boy!

Three

We hear five young girls playing excitedly in a country garden.

Angela 84 (*internal*)   My mum she never had boys. Five girls. No boys. Just girls.

Chatter of five young girls' voices.

Mum   A bobby soxers' club? What's a bobby soxers' club when it's at home?

Don't you gang up on me! You gang up and I'll tell your dad!

Angela 84 (*internal*)   My mum liked having girls. Except when it got too much and then she'd say:

Mum   Why did I have so many fucking girls?

Angela 84 (*internal*)   That's just the way she spoke.

Four

Small kitchen. **Angela** *(aged fifteen) is writing with an ink pen in an exercise book.* **Mum** *is stirring a pot of stew on the oven.*

Mum   What you doing, Rita?

Angela 15   I'm writing.

Mum   What you writing, Rita?

Angela 15   It's a poem.

Mum   Why you writing a poem, Rita? Is it for school?

Angela 15   No not for school.

Mum   Well, could you stop writing your poem please and peel these potatoes?

Angela 15   Mum!

Mum   We're not going to eat poems for our tea are we? (*Pause.*) Rita!

Angela *sighs and starts peeling the potatoes.*

Angela 15   Mum.

Mum   Yes?

Angela 15   I don't want to be called Rita any more.

Mum   Why's that?

Angela 15   I don't like Rita.

Mum   I chose Rita. Rita's a nice name. What's wrong with Rita?

Angela 15   It's just . . . it's

Angela 84 (*internal*)   I wanted to say 'common'.

Angela 15   Just . . .

Angela 84 (*internal*)   But if I said 'common' Mum would have whacked me.

We hear **Mum** *slap* **Angela 15**.

Mum   Don't you get big ideas! Lady Muck!

Angela 84 (*internal*)   So I didn't say 'common'.

Mum   Well, if you don't want to be Rita what do you want to be?

Angela 15   Angela.

Mum   Angela? That's a bit posh. Ange – eh – lah. Ang – eh – lah.

Angela 15   I like it.

Mum   You get on with those potatoes. Angie.

Angela 15 *and* **Angela 84**   It's Angela.

Five

A group of ten people chatting in a village hall.

Director   Good evening! If I could have your attention please, everyone! Good evening.

The chatter dies away.

Thank you to everyone for turning up on this chilly night. The heaters are on so who knows perhaps after a couple of hours' rehearsal we may be able to take off our coats and scarves.

Polite laughter.

When I announced that the Kimpton Village Players' next production would be *Peg o' My Heart* everybody asked me the same question: Who would play Peg? Aren't you all a bit too long in the tooth for anyone to play Peg?

Polite laughter.

And I answered: you're quite right. We don't have a Peg amongst us – we're a bunch of crocks ! (*Response.*) But I'll find us a Peg.

Angela 84 (*internal*)   I wore a tweedy suit that I made from a pattern.

Director   If Hollywood can find a Scarlett O'Hara . . .

Angela 84 (*internal*)   I had a string of pearls. Not real pearls. Woolies' pearls. But they did the job.

Director   And I'm happy to say that tonight we're joined by a newcomer to the Players. Our perfect Peg. Angela Wrightson.

Round of applause.

Plummy Man   Welcome to the Players, Angela.

Angela 15   Thank you very much.

Chatter.

Plummy Woman   I'm having a little tea party on Sunday, Angela.

Angela 84 (*internal*)   The doctor's wife. Calling me Angela.

Plummy Woman   I hope you can join us.

Angela 15   Yes please thank you very much.

Plummy Woman   What would a tea party be without our leading lady?

Angela 84 (*internal*)   Leading lady! Well! You don't let it go to your head.

Director   Righteeho, up on our feet and let's start blocking Act One.

Furniture moved and chatter as everyone prepares to block Act One.

Angela 84 (*internal*)   Peg's an Irish girl. So why I hadn't thought but I hadn't thought. I had to do an Irish accent straight off.

Angela 15 (*poor Irish accent*)   What is it you'll be wanting?

Director   That's a jolly good try, Angela.

Six

Room in a hospital.

Angela (*aged twenty-five*) *is waiting.*

A **Doctor** *enters.*

Doctor   Mrs Ravenhill? Rita Ravenhill?

Angela 25   That's right. That's me. Only I'm called Angela. It says Rita but I'm Angela.

Doctor   Well, Angela I expect you'd like to know the results wouldn't you?

Angela 25   Yes please, doctor.

Doctor   Well, I'm happy to say: baby's all healthy.

Angela 25   Oh that's – thank you – that's very good.

Doctor   What are you hoping for, Angela?

Angela 25   Well, a baby.

Doctor   Ha! Of course a baby yes of course a baby. But a boy or a girl?

Angela 25   Oh I don't know. Either. My husband wants a boy but he'll be happy with a girl. It's not two is it? It is just the one?

Doctor   It is just the one yes.

Angela 25   Oh yes that's good.

Angela 84 (*internal*)   I really wanted a girl

Happiest day

The sun come out and spread through the room

Touched my tum

I could feel the girl

You know what you want to say to her

The things you're going to do with the girl

Suddenly you race through the years ahead

you're going to spend the years with the girl

play games

Run down the road in the rain

Rainfall.

Angela 84   Oooh look, darlin', it's raining. No don't jump in the puddle. Because you'll get all wet if you jump in the puddle.

A **Little Girl** *laughs excitedly and jumps up and down in a puddle.*

Angela 84   Now you've gone and done it. Got yourself all wet. Now what we gonna do? Here's what we'll do. Let's jump in the puddle together. Up and down. Wet through.

She and the **Little Girl** *laugh together and jump up and down in the puddle.*

Suddenly everything is silent.

Angela 84   Only

Only

I let her down

did something wrong

I was wrong

I was made wrong

When they made me they made me wrong

Only a few months to go

Few months more

the girl bled away

I bled the girl away

That's when they told me: it was a girl you lost

Washed away in my

All the future washed away

The rainfall returns and continues throughout:

Angela 84 (*internal*)   Ted wanted a girl

Ted wanted her as much as me

He was angry with me

Made all wrong

He disappears

Because he's so angry with me

Because I'm made all

When I talk about the girl he says

Ted 25   Don't upset yourself, Angie.

Angela 84 (*internal*)   I mustn't upset myself

Only

Only

I do talk to her

We run down the road in the rain

it's all going on

I don't upset myself

But I do like to run with

Did she ever have a name?

Maybe she had a name

Only I've forgotten the

You don't let something like that upset you

You carry on

Little Girl (*phone*)   If they've got walnut cake yes you can have walnut cake.

Angela 84   Oooh, walnut cake that would be lovely. (*Internal.*) I thought it was you speaking to me, darling because I'd forgot that you were washed away but it wasn't you speaking to me it was my son.

Mark 52 (*phone*)   If they've got walnut cake yes you can have walnut cake.

Angela 84   Oooh, walnut cake that would be lovely. Excuse me please who am I speaking to? (*Internal.*) I've got a son.

A boy's alright.

A boy's good isn't it?

Sound of the **Little Girl** *crying.*

Angela 84   Are you a bit jealous, darling?

Don't be silly

Don't be a silly girl

I don't have favourites

love you all just the same.

The rainfall builds and then stops.

Seven

Suburban living room. **Angela** *(aged thirty-four) is hoovering. Radio 2 in the background. She hums along.*

Mark (*aged four*)   Mummy, Mummy!

Angela 34   Wait a minute.

Mark 4   Mummy, I want to –

Angela 34   I'm doing the hoovering.

Mark 4   But I want to.

Angela 84 (*internal*)   He was never slow coming forwards, Mark. Pushy.

Angela 34 *switches off the hoover.*

Angela 34   What is it, darlin'?

Mark 4   I want to do the Jemima dance.

Angela 34   The Jemima dance? Like we saw in the film?

Mark 4   Yes the Jemima dance like in the film.

Angela 84 (*internal*)   There's a film

We've been to the

It's a ballet only it's a film which is based on the books

Lots of stories in it only his favourite is the duck story

I take him down the films when Ted's at work

on your own with a kiddie you've got to break up the day

It's a flea pit really

Still get back in time to cook the tea.

Angela 34   Do you remember the fox Jemima dances with?

Mark 4   No.

Angela 34   You must remember the fox. Dressed all smart but he wants to eat Jemima and her eggs. Bad.

Mark 4   I don't remember that bit.

Angela 34   Well I do – that fox scared the life out of me. If you're going to do the Jemima dance you go out in the garden and practise. Show me later.

Mark 4   Can't.

Angela 34   Why not?

Mark 4   I need a beak. Jemima has a beak.

Angela 34   Alright then let's make you a beak.

Angela 84 (*internal*)   Cardboard cone painted yellow, bit of elastic.

Angela 34   That's a lovely beak. Go out in the garden and do your Jemima dance.

Mark 4 (*slightly muffled by cardboard beak*)   I can't. Jemima has wings.

Angela 84 (*internal*)   Old bed sheet tied to each wrist.

Mark 4   Jemima has yellow legs.

Angela 84 (*internal*)   He's a monster. However much you go along, Mark wants more.

Mark 4   I gotta have yellow legs.

Angela 84 (*internal*)   Old pair of tights. Green but they'll have to do.

Angela 34   You got your legs, your wings, your beak. Do your dance.

Mark 4   I need an egg.

Angela 34   Yeah?

Mark 4   Jemima does the dance round an egg.

Angela 84 (*internal*)   Pushy.

Mark 4   I need a really big egg.

Angela 84 (*internal*)   You love them of course but sometimes as well you

Angela 34   Well, I suppose that's right yes. A really big egg. Shall we make a really big egg?

Mark 4   Yes! How we gonna make a really big egg?

We hear a balloon being blown up, newspaper being torn into strips, flour and water stirred in a bowl.

Angela 84 (*internal*)   Blow up the balloon, newspaper torn into strips, stick it on the balloon with the flour and water, into the airing cupboard and then you paint it white.

Angela 34   That's good. I'd say that looks just like a Jemima egg.

Mark 4   No it doesn't.

Angela 34   Now you take your egg and do the Jemima dance in the garden.

Mark 4   I can't. The egg's all wrong. I don't want to dance with that.

Angela 34   Well, it's the best I can do. You want better you go and find yourself another mummy who can do it better.

She is tearful.

Mark 4   Mummy, why are you crying?

Angela 34   Because I'm silly. That's all.

Eight

A bedroom. **Angela 84** *is searching through boxes of books and papers.*

Angela 84 (*internal*)   Where is it? It's gotta be somewhere. The book's in here somewhere.

When my son comes Saturday he'll want me to read him the Jemima book.

(*Calls.*) Ted! Have you got the book?

Ted!

(*Internal.*) I'll put on a nice blouse for when my son comes. Always cheers you up. Nice blouse.

Where is it?

My son's – oh what's his name?

He's got a fat little face, freckles. Tiny thing.

It's his favourite book.

He was always scared though of the fox.

Come to eat up your eggs.

Sounds of a hospital ward.

Angela 84   When I was on the maternity ward. The birth was hard and I was on the ward and there was a nurse.

The sound of **Angela 84** *searching through the papers continues alongside the hospital ward.*

Nurse One   Would you like to see the baby, Mrs Ravenhill?

Angela 30 (*exhausted*)   Yes please, nurse.

Nurse One   Here we are, Mrs Ravenhill.

Angela 30   Oh.

Nurse One   That's your baby boy, Mrs Ravenhill.

Angela 30   Oh.

Nurse One   Is he your first, Mrs Ravenhill?

Angela 30   He is. Apart from . . . yes. He's my first.

Nurse One   Would you like to hold baby, Mrs Ravenhill?

Angela 30   I don't know. Do most people hold the baby?

Nurse One   Most people do for a moment yes. And as you get stronger, every day you can hold the baby more and more.

Angela 30   Nurse.

Nurse One   Yes, Mrs Ravenhill?

Angela 30   I'm frightened

Nurse One   Lots of people

Angela 30   that I might – I might – lose him. Drop him. Kill him.

Nurse One   lots of people feel like that at first. It's very normal. Hold the baby for a moment.

Angela 30   Yes.

Nurse One *passes the baby to* **Angela**.

Nurse One   There we are.

Angela 84 (*internal*)   The nurse is watching me and I know she wants me to smile. But honestly. That baby. It was so ugly. And when she looked at me she saw on my face disgust.

Nurse One   Shall I take him back now, Mrs Ravenhill?

Angela 30   Please.

Nurse One   Don't you worry, my dear. It's the ugly duckling that grows into the beautiful swan.

The ward fades. **Angela 84** *is searching the papers.*

Angela 84   It's not here. Where's the Jemima book gone?

Where have all the kiddies things gone?

Ted takes it all away and he puts it up the attic.

I gotta get up the attic.

Nine

Angela 84 *drags a stepladder along a carpeted hallway. It's hard work and the sound of her struggle is heard at the same time as her inner thoughts.*

Angela 84 (*internal*)   Jemima lays eggs

Plenty of eggs

They come out of her

Only there's a – what is she?

Wife of the farmer

Farmer's wife says that Jemima can't look after the eggs

She doesn't believe that a duck is the right bird to look after eggs

Well, farmer's wife knows best

I suppose

Takes away the eggs

Gets the hen bird to sit on 'em until they're hatched.

She reaches the spot she wants and sets up the A-frame stepladder.

Angela 84 (*internal*)   Jemima's done the carrying, the laying only now it's the hen does the hatching

Mustn't grumble

Only Jemima doesn't like it

Got to hatch me own eggs

Next time before I lay

Gonna run away from the farm

I'm gonna find a place where I can lay and hatch them all by myself

Get your shawl on, Jemima

Get your bonnet on

Off we go.

(*Calls.*) Ted! I'm going up the attic to find the Jemima book.

During the following, she tries to pull herself up the stepladder but only manages a few steps.

Angela 84 (*internal*)   There's a good place

There amongst the foxgloves you can do your hatching

Show that farmer's wife

I can hatch me own eggs thank you very much

All them eggs taken off me, hatched by the hen

I'm going to put a stop to that

And I'll lay my eggs

And I'll dance my dance

Because I'm happy now that I've got the foxgloves where I can do my hatching

In my bonnet and my shawl

Dancing and dancing and

AGH!

She falls from the ladder. The ladder topples with a crash. She lies on the floor, trying to push herself up.

Angela 84 (*internal*)   Now look what you've done, you stupid old woman. They'll put you in the hospital and then you won't be here Saturday to see your son. My head. Blood.

Rustle of approaching **Fox**.

Angela 84   What's that? Who's there?

Fox (*approaching*)   Hatch your eggs amongst the fox gloves?

Angela 84 (*internal*)   Who's that? The Fox. I don't want to see the Fox. I don't want to see you!

Fox   Oh my dear there's a far better place to hatch your eggs.

Angela 84 (*internal*)   His clothes

He's dressed so smartly

He's a gentleman in that coat

But his black nose and his sharp ears and his teeth and his claws.

Mister Fox.

His voice

Fox   I have a shed where it's warm and it's dry

Where the rain and the wind never come

Hatch your eggs in my shed

(*Retreating.*) Come on.

Ten

Inside a tin shed.

A creaky tin door opens.

Fox   You can hatch your eggs in here.

Angela 84 (*internal*)   Feathers all over the floor

shed full of feathers

Why are there feathers all over the floor?

But when there's no wind and no rain

And his voice is so smooth

You don't listen to yourself and you leave the foxgloves

I can still dance here

Come on, Jemima

Make your nest

And lay your eggs

That's it, Jemima, lovely batch of eggs

We hear **Jemima/Angela** *settle down on the straw over her eggs.*

Fox   Now that you've laid your eggs why don't we have a meal to celebrate?

Let's feast.

Angela 84 (*voice slightly duck-like*)   Oh thank you very much.

Fox   Here's a list of all the herbs I want you to collect so that I can prepare the feast.

Sage and parsley and thyme and

Angela 84   They're the herbs you'd use to stuff a duck.

Fox   Stuff a duck? Oh no, my dear. We shall be feasting on omelette.

A loud ambulance siren.

Eleven

A hospital ward.

Nurse Two   Hello, Rita.

Angela 84 (*internal*)   Rita? Who's Rita?

Nurse Two   Do you know where you are, Rita?

Angela 84 (*internal*)   She thinks I'm Rita.

Nurse Two   You're in the Princess Royal Hospital, Rita.

Angela 84 (*internal*)   I'm Angela.

Nurse Two   You had a nasty fall.

Angela 84   Will I be out Saturday?

Nurse Two   You'll have to ask the doctor about that.

Angela 84   I've got to be out Saturday. My son's coming Saturday.

Nurse Two   Let's see what the doctor says. Get some rest now, Rita.

Hospital ward acoustic continues. A baby cries in the distance.

Angela 84 (*internal*)   Lost the girl.

My body couldn't hold it.

Then I lost again and again.

Too early to know if it was boys or girls.

Nothing stayed.

Expectation and then blood.

A lot of

You don't think you can do any more.

You're just made wrong and that's that.

There are people who are happy with no kiddies.

They say they're happy.

Only I don't believe them.

I don't believe there's anyone who's happy who doesn't have a kiddie.

Sound of children playing.

Angela 84 (*internal*)   You can talk to other people's kiddies.

Play with them, little treats.

But you're always wanting to steal their kiddies.

That's an awful thing to want.

What sort of awful person wants to steal kiddies?

I know I'm bad but that's a worse feeling than I ever thought I had.

Nurse Two (*internal*)   Watch out for that Angie – she's a kiddie stealer.

Angela 84 (*internal*)   I'd never get Ted to agree to that.

He's a good man.

Adoption is an option.

I think that would be nice.

Look after a kid someone else didn't want.

Bring them up.

It's different but that's as good as your own kid.

I'd break the rules and tell them that they were my own.

Mark 4   I want to do the Jemima dance.

Angela 84   You're my kid and I'm your mummy.

Baby cries over sound of children playing.

Angela 84 (*internal*)   The girl wouldn't like it but she's dead so she'll just have to hold her tongue.

Sound of children playing fades.

Twelve

Suburban bedroom. **Angela 34** *lies on the bed. In the distance* **Mark 4** *can be heard laughing.*

Angela 34 (*internal*)   Mark's always pushing

Thing about Mark is he always wants more

Gives me a migraine

I tell him play by yourself

He's got the tights, the wings, the beak, the egg

I come in here and I lie on the bed.

Mark 4 (*approaching*)   Mummy, Mummy.

Angela 34   What now, Mark? I've got a migraine.

Angela 84 (*internal*)   You want the kiddie

And then half the time you wished you never had

Only you don't let them see that

always got to put on a performance for Mark.

Mark 4   Mummy, Jemima has a bonnet and a shawl.

Angela 34   Does she?

Mark 4   Look here's the picture in the book. Bonnet and shawl.

Angela 34   I can't see it now 'cos of my migraine.

Mark 4   I've got to have a bonnet and a shawl.

Angela 34   I've got to stay in the bed in the dark until I'm better.

Mark 4   Where am I going to get my bonnet and my shawl?

Angela 84 (*internal*)   Always wants more.

Mark 4   When's Daddy coming home?

Thirteen

Kitchen. **Angela 34** *is washing up while at the kitchen table.* **Ted 34** *is reading to* **Mark 4** *from* The Wind in the Willows.

Ted 34   And then, in that utter clearness of the imminent dawn, while Nature, flushed with fullness of incredible colour, seemed to hold her breath for the event, Mole looked in the very eyes of the Friend and Helper; saw the backward sweep of the curved horns, gleaming in the growing daylight

From now on **Ted 34** *continues to read under* **Angela 34**'s *internal monologue – see below.*

Ted 34   saw the stern, hooked nose between the kindly eyes that were looking down on them humourously, while the bearded mouth broke into a half-smile at the corners; saw the rippling muscles on the arm that lay across the broad chest, the long supple hand still holding the pan-pipes only just fallen away from the parted lips; saw the splendid curves of the shaggy limbs disposed in majestic ease on the sward

Angela 84 (*internal, same time as* **Ted 34**)   Ted comes home at night

He does the bath, reads the story

I do the washing-up

Pause.

Ted loves the bath and the story

Round and round they go

Pause.

Again and again

Pause.

Wind in the sodding Willows

Pause.

Days are so long.

Ted 34 *continues reading after* **Angela 34** *internal monologue.*

Ted 34   saw, last of all, nestling between his very hooves, sleeping soundly in entire peace and contentment, the little, round, podgy, childish form of the baby otter. All this he saw, for one moment breathless and intense, vivid on the morning sky; and still, as he looked, he lived; and still, as he lived, he wondered.

Angela 34   Look, Ted. Mark's fallen asleep.

We hear **Mark 4**'s *sleeping breath.*

Fourteen

The hospital ward.

Angela 84 (*calls out*)   Doctor! Doctor! Where's the Doctor?

Nurse Two (*approaches*)   The doctor isn't here, Rita.

Angela 84   I need to speak to the doctor.

Nurse Two   It's three in the morning.

Angela 84   When can I see the doctor?

A groan from another bed.

Nurse Two   Rita – you've woken up the other ladies.

Angela 84   Is the doctor coming?

Nurse Two   The doctor's been.

Angela 84   When?

Nurse Two   Today.

Angela 84   Why didn't he speak to me?

Nurse Two   He did speak to you, Rita. Only you've forgotten.

Angela 84   I wouldn't forget that.

Nurse Two   You have memory problems, Rita.

Angela 84   Do I? I don't like the sound of that.

Nurse Two   It's nothing to worry about. You're safe here.

Angela 84   Did the doctor say I can go home Saturday?

Nurse Two   Get some sleep, Rita.

Angela 84   Did he say I can go home Saturday to see my son?

Nurse Two   The doctor said you have to stay another week.

Angela 84   Sod off, you bloody bitch.

Nurse Two   Rita!

Angela 84   Stop calling me Rita. No one calls me Rita. I'm Angela.

Fifteen

A suburban hallway.

Mark 4   Daddy! Daddy! I'm ready!

Ted 34   What about your beak?

Mark 4   I couldn't get it on.

Ted 34   Shall I help you get the beak on?

Mark 4   Yes.

Ted 34   Stand still. I'm going to tie the elastic and . . . there we are.

Mark 4   Do I look like Jemima?

Ted 34   Just like Jemima. Are you ready to go?

Mark 4   Did you get the film?

Ted 34   Here in the camera.

Angela 34 (*approaching*)   What are you two up to?

Ted 34   We're going out.

Angela 34   Where you going?

Ted 34   A walk in the woods.

Angela 34   In his Jemima costume?

Ted 34   That's what he wants to do.

Angela 34   Why do you want to wear your Jemima costume to the woods?

Mark 4   We're going to make a film.

Angela 34   Are you? What film you going to make?

Mark 4   A Jemima film. I'm going to do the Jemima dance and Daddy's going to film it.

Angela 34   Is that right?

Ted 34   It's what he wants to do.

Angela 34   It's going to rain.

Ted 34   Think so?

Angela 34   Course it's going to rain. Look out the window. A lot of rain on the way.

Mark 4   I can do the Jemima dance in the rain.

Angela 34   Your egg'll melt in the rain. Can't you go another day?

Mark 4   No! Today!

Angela 34   Well, get the umbrella and the wellies then and don't blame me if your egg melts.

Mark 4 (*retreats*)   Yes, Mummy.

Angela 34   Can I come with you?

Ted 34   To the woods?

Angela 34   To the woods yes.

Ted 34   I thought you had a migraine.

Angela 34   It's almost gone now.

Ted 34   I thought if I took him out you'd have some peace and quiet.

Angela 34   Getting out the house would do me good.

Ted 34   Alright then. If you like. I just thought . . .

Angela 34   Yes?

Ted 34   We could show you the film later. Once it's developed and I've done the editing.

Angela 34   You'd rather I stayed at home?

Ted 34   No only – come with us and what will you do, Angie?

Angela 34   What will I do?

Ted 34   He'll be dancing and I'll be filming. What will you do?

Angela 84 (*internal*)   It wasn't you took him to see the film, it wasn't you watched him day after day practising his Jemima dance, it's not your tights he's wearing, it wasn't you who made his beak and his egg. Only I didn't say any of that.

Angela 34   What will I do? Well I, suppose, I'll watch.

Sixteen

Angela 84 (*internal*)   There was a song. Called 'Peg o' My Heart'.

It wasn't in the play but I think it was something to do with the play.

Maybe the song came first.

Or maybe it was the play came first.

When the song come on the radio Mum would say:

Mum   Oooh, Ange – eh – la. They're playing your song.

Angela 84 (*internal*)   And she'd laugh.

All the way through the song.

Thought I was getting too big for my boots.

Her way of saying: Pride comes before a fall.

I didn't like the song anyway.

Stupid song. La la la la la.

We hear the audience in the village hall clapping, cheering, wolf whistling. Continues under:

Angela 84 (*internal*)   Once it was in the newspaper that I was the leading lady they all started singing that song to me. Outside the pub, beer in their hands. Dad and his mates. Kids up the Sunday school. I walked away. Soon as they started. wouldn't say anything. Just walk away.

Angela 15 (*internal*)   I can't be bothered with the likes of you.

I got lines to learn.

The clapping and cheering builds.

Seventeen

Persistent ring of an electric door bell. **Angela** *(aged thirty) opens the front door.*

Woman   Mrs Ravenhill?

Angela 30   Yes?

Woman   Mrs Rita Ravenhill?

Angela 30   I'm Angela.

Woman   Is Mrs Rita Ravenhill at home?

Angela 30   I'm Rita and I'm Angela. I was born Rita but I'm called Angela.

Woman   I see yes. Would you like me to amend our records?

Angela 30   If you could. What records?

Woman   You got the letter saying that I'd call this morning?

Angela 30   I'm not sure.

Woman   From the adoption services.

Angela 30   Oh that letter. Yes of course. Come in. I'll put the kettle on.

Eighteen

Suburban living room. **Angela 30** *approaches with a tray of tea and biscuits.*

Angela 30   It's only biscuits.

Woman   Not for me thank you.

Angela 30   I meant to get cake only . . .

Woman   There's no need.

Angela 30   What with one thing and another.

Woman   Of course. Just tea for me.

Angela 30   With sugar?

Woman   I use a sweetener.

Angela 30   I've got some somewhere.

Woman   I've brought my own.

Angela 30   Alright then.

Woman   No milk.

Angela 30   No milk?

Woman   No thank you.

Angela 30   I've never had it without milk. Is it nice?

Woman   I like it. Sometimes with lemon.

Angela 30   Lemon? Really?

Uneasy silence as **Angela 30** *pours two teas, hands one to the* **Woman** *and her dispenser clicks two sweeteners into the tea.*

Angela 30   Watching your figure are you?

Woman   I try to.

Angela 30   I should do that. I mean most of the time I'm good as gold. But I do like a biscuit with my tea.

Uneasy silence as they drink their tea and **Angela 30** *eats her biscuit.*

Woman   Will your husband be joining us?

Angela 30   Ted?

Woman   Yes will Ted be joining us?

Angela 30   He's at work.

Woman   At work? But it did say in the letter

Angela 30   Did it?

Woman   Yes it did say in the letter that I needed to meet husband and wife together. Did you read that part of the letter?

Angela 30   I suppose I must have.

Woman   Are you serious about adoption, Mrs Ravenhill?

Angela 30   Sorry. I've wasted your time.

Woman   It's important that you read our letters very carefully.

Angela 30   Yes of course. Sorry, sorry.

Woman   I will need to talk to you both as husband and wife.

Angela 30   Ted doesn't get back until after five. Can you come back then?

Woman   Since I'm here why don't you show me around? I'd like to see the room you've put aside for baby and the bathing and cooking facilities.

Angela 30   There's no need. I don't want to waste any more of your time.

Woman   It said in the letter that we'd need to see –

Angela 30   Did it? I suppose that's right. Only . . .

Woman   Mrs Ravenhill?

Angela 30   We were very serious about adoption. Been trying for nearly ten years for one of our own. Only I miscarried them.

Woman   I'm sorry.

Angela 30   You think your body can't do it don't you?

Woman   Of course.

Angela 30   And we moved here so there'd be a room for a baby so we thought adopt only . . .

Woman   Yes?

Angela 30   I forgot you were coming. The letter was sent months ago and since then – I should have telephoned but since you sent the letter – I'm having a baby. Just started my fifth month. I meant to cancel but what with everything I – I'm really very sorry.

Woman   Oh that's wonderful news. Congratulations, Angela.

Angela 84 (*internal*)   I expected her to say 'You've wasted my time, you silly cow' but she didn't. She was really nice.

Woman   It happens all the time. Lots of ladies once they've started the adoption process, it takes the pressure off and they conceive all by themselves.

Angela 30   Oh no. Not all by myself. It was Ted done it as well.

Woman   Well, yes indeed Ted played his part I'm sure.

Angela 30   Ted wants a boy and he wants to call him Mark.

Woman   And what do you want, Angela?

Nineteen

Hospital ward.

Ted 84   Angie? You awake, Angie? Only me.

Angela 84   Ted?

Ted 84   How you feeling?

Angela 84   Alright. When am I getting out?

Ted 84   I don't know. What did the doctor say?

Angela 84   I don't know. I hate it here. It's all old ladies.

Ted 84   I brought your biscuits.

Angela 84   I don't want a biscuit.

Ted 84   It's your favourites.

Angela 84   I want to go home.

Ted 84   Have a biscuit.

Angela 84   No.

Ted 84   Alright then I'll have a biscuit.

We hear him tear open the packet and eat several biscuits as:

Angela 84 (*internal*)   He's such an old man now

Look at him

When I met Ted he was so good looking.

Oooh, he was handsome.

I couldn't get over it.

It was – honestly – lust.

A dance hall.

Angela 84 (*internal*)   There was lots of apprentices at the dance but Ted was the only one I had eyes for.

Lots of girls dancing with him.

So many girls.

Not me.

He didn't even look at me.

Then they said:

Voice on Mic   The next dance is the ladies excuse me.

Angela 84 (*internal*)   So of course I was straight up to him and:

Angela 18   Excuse me.

Angela 84 (*internal*)   And we danced to the band.

And after I said:

Angela 18   So when am I going to see you again?

Angela 84 (*internal*)   I had to see him again straight away.

The next day.

A bicycle being pedalled furiously as dance hall fades.

Angela 84 (*internal*)   I stole my sister's bike, cycled out the village, through the lanes, up to the factory – met him at the gates.

Ted 84   Hello, Angela.

Angela 18   Hello, Ted. Fancy seeing you here.

Ted 84   Where you going?

Angela 18   Round to your digs. For tea.

Ted 84   Yeah?

Angela 18   Unless you've got another girl coming round?

Ted 84   No only I share my room.

Angela 18   Who with?

Ted 84   Another apprentice.

Angela 18   Couldn't he go for a walk?

Ted 84   I could ask him.

Angela 18   Yeah ask him to go for a really long walk.

Ted 84   Alright then. I will.

Angela 84 (*internal*)   Mum thought I was moving too fast.

Mum   You want to slow down, my girl.

Angela 84 (*internal*)   I didn't want to slow down.

I wanted to start courting straight away.

Cycled over every evening.

Even faster pedalling then fades away.

Angela 84 (*internal*)   One day we were in the kitchen at home.

Me and Julie and Mum.

Mum, **Angela 18** *and* **Julie 16** *are doing the washing-up together.*

Angela 84 (*internal*)   And Julie said

She knew the answer

I'm sure she knew the answer but she wanted to embarrass Mum.

Julie 16   Mum, what's a virgin?

Angela 84 (*internal*)   And Mum looked straight at Julie

Didn't look at me, looked straight at Julie:

Mum   A virgin is what you are and your sister isn't.

Angela 84 (*internal*)   Mum knew how to hurt when she wanted to.

Dig in the knife.

The hospital ward acoustic returns, **Ted 84** *munching a biscuit.*

Ted 84   Mark phoned.

Angela 84   Yeah?

Ted 84   He said he spoke to you a few days ago. Called you at home. Before your fall.

Angela 84   I don't remember.

Ted 84   Said he spoke to you and said he'd take you out for a walk through the woods and have some walnut cake.

Angela 84   Walnut cake. Yes please. I like walnut cake.

Ted 84   I told him that you had a fall and that you were in the Princess Royal.

Angela 84   Oh, Ted, don't tell everyone.

Ted 84   I haven't told everyone.

Angela 84   I don't want everyone knowing my business.

Ted 84   I told Mark. He's coming to the hospital Saturday.

Angela 84   Is he? Who is this Mark?

Ted 84   You know who Mark is.

Angela 84   Do I?

Ted 84   Of course you do.

Angela 84   Well, if you say I do then I suppose I must do mustn't I?

Ted 84   You're just being silly now, Angie.

Angela 84   Silly, am I silly?

Ted 84   You know Mark's your son.

Angela 84   I never had a son just a daughter and she died.

Ted 84   That's not right. That's silly. Stop saying all these silly things.

Angela 84   Bugger off, you horrible old man!

Ted 84   Come on, Angie. You're upsetting yourself.

Angela 84   It's you upsets me. Take your biscuits and go. I don't want to see you again.

Ted 84   Don't. They're all listening.

Angela 84   Nosy bitches. All of you!

Twenty

The woods. Bird song.

Angela 84 (*internal*)   Sat there on a log and Mark's telling Ted what to do.

Mark 4   You stand over there with the camera and I'm going to be over here and when I go over there you move the camera like this.

Angela 84 (*internal*)   And on he goes.

In the distance, **Ted** *and* **Mark** *make the film of the Jemima dance. Rainfall begins and builds during:*

Angela 84 (*internal*)   Rain's started now.

I knew it would.

You do sometimes wonder:

What would it be like if I could have held on to the girl?

Silly.

There we go.

She could have been difficult.

She could have been a right little cow.

We could have rowed all the time.

I gave my mum a terrible time.

I wasn't a good girl.

I think you'd understand a girl.

A dad understands a boy and a mum understands a girl.

Those tights are covered in mud.

I'll need to rinse them.

Soon as we get home.

Angela 34 (*calls*)   There's biscuits and Ribena if you want them.

Angela 84 (*internal*)   One day when Ted was at work I took Mark up the pictures. *The Tales of Beatrix Potter*.

But we had to leave the pictures because I wasn't feeling well.

And when we got outside I was sick in the street.

I lay down on a bench, one hand on my head and one hand on my stomach.

And Mark touched me and he said:

Mark 4   What is it, Mummy? What's happening?

Angela 34   Don't worry, Mark. It's nothing. Soon be better again.

Angela 84 (*internal*)   You think when you've waited so long – you think when your body's let you down so many times – you think when the baby comes – when Mark's born – you think that it's going to be a happy ending.

Silly to think that but you do.

I wanted to be happy. For him. Lovely little boy.

But not long after he came along . . . I suppose they'd call it depression. All through my body.

Policeman   Everything alright, love?

Angela 84   Policeman.

Angela 34   It's just a migraine. Soon be better again.

Policeman   This your boy?

Angela 34   That's right.

Policeman   What's your name, son?

Mark 4   Mark.

Policeman   You look after your mum, Mark.

Mark 4   Don't worry, Mummy. Soon be better again.

Angela 84 (*internal*)   The migraines happened again – sometimes we'd be at home or sometimes at the shops and I'd lie on a bench.

Acoustic of the woods and rain returns.

Angela 34 (*calls*)   Home soon. Your egg won't take the rain much longer.

Twenty-One

Suburban living room.

Mark 4   Where's Mummy?

Ted 34   She's not well. She's lying down on the bed. Where you going?

Mark 4   Upstairs to see Mummy.

Ted 34   You can't go up there. She has to be left alone.

Mark 4   I want to see her.

Ted 34   No! Your mummy's very ill. The doctor's been. She's had a heart attack.

Mark 4   What's a heart attack?

Ted 34   It means her heart doesn't work properly. She mustn't put any strain on her heart.

Mark 4   What if we're just on time for the train but we have to run up the stairs?

Ted 34   You'll have to wait for the next train. She must never run up stairs ever again. From now on you must be good all the time and never do anything that puts a strain on Mummy's heart.

Twenty-Two

Bedroom.

Angel 34 *lies on the bed, her breathing laboured.*

The bedroom door opens and **Mark 4** *comes over to the bed.*

Mark 4   Mummy.

Angela 34 (*tender*)   Oh Mark.

Angela 84 (*internal*)   He didn't mean to make me ill. He didn't understand. Just a kiddy. I wanted a baby. Even if it killed me.

Twenty-Three

A church hall.

We hear an excited audience including many children waiting for a performance to start.

Angela 84 (*internal*)   When I saw it in the local paper, I thought ooh, Mark'll love that.

The sound of the audience falls back but doesn't completely disappear under:

Suburban living room.

Angela 34 (*offers newspaper*)   Look at this, Mark. See what they're doing at Christmas? Can you read it?

Mark 4   No.

Angela 34   I bet you can.

Mark 4   I can't.

Angela 34   You can if you make out the sounds of the letters. Put your finger under the letters as you go along and say the sounds.

Mark 4   Can I have my tea?

Angela 34   After you've done this.

Mark 4   Alright. Wuh.

Angela 34   Good.

Mark 4   Ih.

Angela 34   Wuh, Ih.

Mark 4   Un, Duh.

Angela 34   Altogether.

Mark 4   Wuh, Ih, Un, Duh.

Angela 34   And altogether that's WuhIhUnDuh. Say it fast.

Mark 4   Wind?

Angela 34   Yes! Oooh, you're a clever little boy. You'll be cleverer than me any day now. New word.

Mark 4   Ih, Nuh. In!

Angela 34   Yes. New word.

Mark 4   Tuh. Huh. Eh. Is it 'the'?

Angela 34   Yes Wind – in – the . . .

Mark 4   Is it Wind in the Willows?

Angela 34   Yes it's a play of the book and they're doing it down by the station this Christmas. Shall we go?

Mark 4   Yes!

Ted 34 (*distant*)   I'm home!

Mark 4   Daddy! Daddy!

Ted 34 (*approaches*)   How's my lovely family tonight? Big kiss for my lovely wife (*kiss*) and a big kiss for my lovely son (*kiss*).

Mark 4   Daddy, they're doing a play of *Wind in the Willows*!

Ted 34   Are they? Where's that then?

Angela 34   In the scout hut down by the station.

Mark 4   Can we go now?

Angela 34   You'll have to wait. It's not on for another three weeks. There's a phone number. Shall I phone and book us three tickets?

Mark 4   Yes.

Ted 34   Not for me. You two go.

Angela 34   Oh go on, Ted. Come with us. It'll be nice.

Ted 34   I don't fancy it.

Angela 34   Why not?

Ted 34   Because a play's never as good as the book is it?

Angela 34   Spoilsport.

Under the following from **Angela 84** *we can hear* **Angela 34** *making the telephone booking.*

Angela 84 (*internal*)   It was an old yellow book of *Wind in the Willows* that someone gave Ted when he was a boy.

His favourite book.

He practised reading it to a kiddie before we even had a kiddie.

And as soon as Mark could understand, Ted would give him his bath every night and then read to him out of *Wind in the Willows*.

So then it was Mark's favourite book as well.

And Ted could do all the voices. Each of them would have a different voice.

Ted 34 (*as* **Toad**)   Glorious, stirring sight! The poetry of motion! The real way to travel! The only way to travel! Here today –in next week tomorrow! Villages skipped, towns and cities jumped – always somebody else's horizon! O bliss! O poop-poop! O my! O my!

Angela 84 (*internal*)   Badger, Mole, Ratty, Toad.

None of them had the same voice.

I could never do that.

Angela 15 (*Irish accent*)   What is it you'll be wanting?

Director   That's a jolly good try, Angela.

Angela 84   To Mark it was like a magic trick. All these different voices coming out of his daddy's mouth. He couldn't believe it.

Sometimes I'd listen at the bedroom door. Didn't go in. It was their special time.

Angela 34 (*approaching*)   All done. Two tickets for the Wednesday. Right then who's ready for their tea?

The sound of the excited audience in the church hall builds.

Angela 84 (*internal*)   All the littlest children were mice and they came a-carolling to Toad Hall.

The tallest boy was Toad.

He stood at the centre of the stage and he had a green stocking over his head.

Which turned his face green and squished his nose.

He looked just like a toad.

Ten-Year-Old Boy as Toad   Glorious, stirring sight! The poetry of motion! The real way to travel! The only way to travel! Here today – in next week tomorrow! Villages skipped, towns and cities jumped – always somebody else's horizon! O bliss! O poop-poop! O my! O my!

Angela 84 (*internal*)   And I looked at Mark and I said:

Angela 34 (*whisper*)   Is that what you want to do, Mark? To stand on the stage with a green stocking over your head?

Mark 4   Yes, Mummy.

Angela 84 (*internal*)   You can't stop Mark. Once he's got an idea in his head he's going to do it and you better not stand in his way.

And the week after, that's when Mark made up the Jemima dance.

Twenty-Four

Hospital car park. Night. Wind and rain.

Angela 84 *is walking across the car park with considerable effort.*

Nurse Two (*distant*)   Angela! Angela!

Angela 84 (*mutters*)   Leave me alone.

Nurse Two (*distant*)   Are you there, Angela?

Angela 84 (*mutters*)   I've got a cruise to go on.

Nurse Two (*distant*)   I've come to take you back to the ward, Angela! The doctor's worried about you! Angela!

We hear a pack of dogs growling and barking, ready to attack. We hear further sounds as **Angela 84** *narrates them.*

Angela 84 (*internal*)

First the dogs were growling, barking.

Fox was barking back at them.

Then Jemima heard teeth ripping at the flesh.

Then she heard great squeals of pain.

Then it got savage: screaming and biting and tearing and barking and howling and roaring and cracking and crunching.

Jemima was frightened.

But she was excited too.

Then the door of the shed flew open and in came the collie and the two fox hounds.

Their mouths all bloody.

And there was fox fur under their claws.

And the coolie dog had a great chunk missing out of his ear.

Jemima knew that they had killed the fox.

And that made her happy.

Nurse Two (*approaching*)   Angela! There you are! You had us worried.

Angela 84   Did I? Why's that then?

Nurse Two   Wandering out in the car park. You could get run over.

Angela 84   Course I wouldn't. I'm not stupid.

Nurse Two   We're getting wet Angela. Come back inside.

Angela 84   You go back. I've got to, I'm going to . . .

Nurse Two   Where are you going, Angela?

Angela 84 (*tearful*)   I don't remember. Why can't I remember?

Nurse Two   Come on, Angela. Don't upset yourself.

Angela 84   I'm frightened.

Nurse Two   Would you like me to hold your hand?

Angela 84   Yes please.

Nurse Two   Shall we walk back now?

Angela 84   Alright.

(*Internal.*) That's the happy ending.

In the ballet it all ends happy.

The dogs get rid of the fox.

But that's not the story.

I don't like it when they change the story.

I wish they'd stick to the story.

In the story the fox hounds are still wild from the fight and they see Jemima's eggs that she's laid and they gobble them all up – each and every one of them.

Until Jemima's got no more eggs.

That's how it is if you do the story properly.

Twenty-Five

Tea rooms. A few customers at tables. **Ted 18** *sits dolefully stirring his tea.*

With the ring of the bell over the door, **Angela 18** *rushes in.*

Angela 18 (*approaching*)   Oh, Ted, I'm sorry.

Ted 18   I was worried about you, Angela.

Angela 18   I got a puncture. Got out the village but then – it went all flat and I had to push the bike all the way here.

Ted 18   I thought it was an accident.

Angela 18   You're a worrier aren't you?

Ted 18   Am I?

Angela 18   Yes you are great big worrier.

Ted 18   Maybe that's because . . .

Angela 18   Yes?

Ted 18   I miss you when you're not here.

Angela 18   Oh Ted.

She kisses him.

Angela 18   You've gone red.

Ted 18   We shouldn't. In public. Kissing in public it's –

She kisses him again.

Ted 18   Angela!

Angela 18   I'm a wicked woman aren't I?

Waiter (*approaches*)   What you having, love?

Angela 18   I hadn't thought.

Waiter   You have to order something or you're out.

Angela 18   Alright then I'll have a tea.

Waiter   That it?

Angela 18   And an iced bun.

Waiter   Iced bun. Thank you. And no more of the canoodling. This is a nice place and we want to keep it that way. (*Retreating*.) Dot – tea and an iced bun on six.

Ted 18   Now look what you've done!

Angela 18   I can't help it when you're so handsome.

Ted 18   What do you want to do tonight?

Angela 18   Well . . .

Ted 18   They've got *Oklahoma!* at the pictures.

Angela 18   That's nice.

Ted 18   Or we can just go for a walk to the reservoir and back?

Angela 18   Ted.

Ted 18   I don't mind.

Angela 18   I can't tonight.

Ted 18   But you said –

Angela 18   I know but I've got rehearsals tonight.

Ted 18   We were supposed

Angela 18   I got my days muddled.

Waiter (*delivering tea*)   Tea and bun. Pay at the door.

Angela 18   Thank you very much.

Waiter (*retreating*)   No dogs inside thank you.

Angela 18 *puts sugar into her tea, stirs. Uneasy silence.*

Angela 18   Ted? Ted? Are you sulking. You are, aren't you? you're sulking.

Ted 18   Do you love me, Angela?

Angela 18   Course I love you.

Ted 18   I want us to be together.

Angela 18   So do I.

Ted 18   For ever.

Angela 18   For ever? You never said for ever before.

Ted 18   I'm saying it now.

Angela 18   Forever yes I'd like for ever very much.

Ted 18   But you're always up the Players rehearsing.

Angela 18   After Peg, they keep on giving me parts.

Ted 18   I don't see you for weeks on end.

Angela 18   Only when there's a show.

Ted 18   If you're serious – about us – I want you to give up the Players.

Angela 18   No!

Ted 18   How we going to be together if you're always up the Players?

Angela 18   Well . . . there's an answer to that.

Twenty-Six

Wings of the village hall stage. An excited audience can be heard 'out front'.

Angela 18   How you getting on?

Ted 18   Not so bad.

Angela 18   Have you been sick again?

Ted 18   I thought I was but in the end nothing came up.

Angela 18   I was like that my first show.

Ted 18   Yeah?

Angela 18   But when you get on there.

Ted 18   I tried running my lines. Toilet. They wouldn't come.

Angela 18   Everything's alright once you're out there. Once you've got the audience it all sort of flies.

Ted 18   I hope you're right.

Plummy Man (*passing*)   Angela! Ted! Here we all are. Break a leg!

Angela 18   You too. Break a leg.

Ted 18   Are you scared?

Angela 18   Excited.

Plummy Woman   Angela, you're wearing a ring.

Angela 18   Yes do you like it?

Plummy Woman   It's just what she would wear isn't it?

Angela 18   What who would wear?

Plummy Woman   Your character.

Angela 18   Oh no this is my ring. Ted gave it to me. Today.

Plummy Woman   So it's your –

Angela 18   Engagement ring yes.

Plummy Woman   Oh, Angela! Congratulations! And Ted this is wonderful –

Ted 18 (*pushing past*)   Excuse me.

Plummy Woman   Is he alright?

Angela 18   He thinks he's going to be sick but he won't be.

Director (*approaches*)   Well, here we are everyone. Nothing left for a useless old producer to do now. All up to you. The

Herald are in tonight although they promised not to come until Thursday so pick up the cues, anticipate your entrances and enjoy yourselves!

Angela 84 (*internal*)   And the *Herald* said: 'Edward Ravenhill and Angela Wrightson as the young lovers are charming.'

Twenty-Seven

Hospital ward.

Ted 84   Here you go, Angie.

Angela 84   What's that?

Ted 84   Cup of tea for you.

Angela 84   No thank you.

Ted 84   Cup of boiling water and a tea bag on the side so you can do it just the way you like it.

Angela 84   I don't want it.

Ted 84   You've got to keep your fluids up or they'll put you on the drip again.

Angela 84   Why are you here, Ted?

Ted 84   Because you're my lovely wife.

Angela 84   I don't want you here.

Ted 84   The house is quiet without you.

Angela 84   Huh.

Ted 84   You looking forward to seeing Mark tomorrow?

Angela 84   I phoned the police station.

Ted 84   Do you think he'll bring walnut cake?

Angela 84   Why do you think I phoned the police station, eh? I'll tell you why. I told the police all about you. What you've been up to.

Ted 84   Don't be silly, Angie.

Angela 84   They'll put you in prison. Rest of your days. That's what they do to murderers.

Ted 84   Drink your tea while it's still hot.

Angela 84   Oh yes you'd like that wouldn't you? Drink the tea so you can poison me.

Ted 84   Silly!

Angela 84   Why do you hate me so much? Why do you want to kill me? Why have you put poison in my tea? Did you pay the doctors to take me away and lock me up here? How long's it been going on? You've been trying to kill me for years.

Fox   Here's a list of all the herbs I want you to collect so that I can prepare the feast.

Angela 84   HELP ME! SOMEONE HELP ME! TED'S GOING TO KILL ME! THIS IS AN EMERGENCY! SOMEONE HELP ME NOW!

Ted 84   Angie! Stop it!

Angela 84   Don't you touch me! HELP! MURDER!

Ted 84   Angie! No! You mustn't.

Angela 84   You have the tea!

She throws the cup of boiling water in his face. He screams in pain.

Ted 84   AGHHH!

Nurse Two (*approaching rapidly*)   Now then what's going on here?

Angela 84   None of your business.

Ted 84 (*in pain*)   There's been an accident. I had an accident.

Nurse Two   Are you hurt, Mr Ravenhill?

Ted 84   I had a shock. Hot tea. I –

Angela 84   Don't lie to her, Ted. He's such a liar.

Ted 84   I spilt the tea over myself.

Nurse Two   I saw Angela throw –

Ted 84   No no.

Nurse Two   If you'd like to clean up – someone at the nurses' station will help you.

Ted 84   Oh yes. (*Retreats.*) Thank you very much.

Angela 84   Don't come back! Evil old man!

Nurse Two   Now then, Angela.

Nurse Two *pulls the curtain around the bed.*

Nurse Two   What's going on, eh? What's upsetting you, Angela?

Angela 84   You know what's been going on.

Nurse Two   No I don't know what's going on. If I did I wouldn't be asking, would I?

Angela 84   You're part of it.

Nurse Two   Part of what?

Angela 84   I don't know how you live with that. Murdering old ladies. How can you do it? (*Becoming very upset.*) MURDERING BITCH!

Nurse Two   I know everything's very confused at the moment.

Angela 84   I'm not confused.

Nurse Two   It's strange being in the hospital. But we'll soon have you home.

Angela 84   And let Ted poison me? You'd like that wouldn't you?

Nurse Two   We all want you to be safe, Angela.

Angela 84   I don't feel safe and you're a liar.

Nurse Two   Time you took your pills. They'll help to calm you down.

Angela 84   I'm not taking any pills.

Nurse Two   Come on, Angela. Sip of water and swallow them down.

Angela 84   I'm NOT TAKING YOUR PILLS! I'M NOT TAKING POISON!

Nurse Two   Just a tiny sip.

Angela 84   GET AWAY FROM ME!

She punches **Nurse Two** *in the face.*

Nurse Two   Oh, Angela! That hurt!

Angela 84   BITCH!

Nurse Two   Hello! Can I have some assistance here please! Immediately!

Angela 84   YOU'RE ALL A PART OF IT! MURDERERS!

Twenty-Eight

Suburban garden.

Angela 30 *opens the back door of the house.*

Angela 30   You can smoke out here, Julie.

Julie 28   I can wait til I'm in the car if you'd rather.

Angela 30   It's alright. I've got a saucer. So you can do your ash.

Julie 28 (*coming out to garden*)   I should have brought an ash tray.

Angela 30   That's alright.

Julie 28   Well, go on then. I'm gasping.

She takes cigarettes and lighter out of her handbag, lights a cigarette, takes a long drag as:

Angela 84 (*internal*)   Julie had boys. Before I could tell her I'd lost the girl, she told me she was expecting.

Julie 28   Ooooh, that's better. You've got a shed, Angie.

Angela 30   That's Ted.

Julie 28   When did you get a shed?

Angela 30   Ted put it up last year. He's in there all the time now. Still, means I get the house to myself most of the time.

Julie 28   You've done the house lovely.

Angela 30   We like it.

Julie 28   Kiddies only mess that up. I'm always saying to Pete: remember how lovely our house was before the kiddies come along and messed it all up? Have my kids messed up your house?

Angela 30   Oh no they've been good as gold.

Julie 28   Wish they were good as gold for me. Oh I almost forgot. (*Searches in handbag.*) We got you a present.

Angela 30   You shouldn't have done that.

Julie 28   An ornament. For looking after the kids.

Angela 84 (*internal*)   Lovely little boys they were. Almost like I had my own.

Julie 28   Here you are.

Angela 30   That's nice. What is it? Is it a bull?

Julie 28   Yes we got it when we went to the bull fight.

Angela 30   Did you go to a bull fight?

Julie 28   Well, you got to go to a bull fight haven't you?

Angela 30   Did they kill a bull?

Julie 28   Almost.

Angela 30   I don't think I'd like that. What's the bull done to deserve that?

Angela 84 (*internal*)   They're killing kiddies now. And there's no one to stop them. There's no one left. Police. Doctors. Neighbours. Husband. All of them – ganged up. On your own. They lock you up in the hospital. Tell you you've got no memory. Tell you you're a mad old woman. They're killing the kiddies and they'll kill you. You got to make it stop.

Twenty-Nine

Hospital ward.

Angela 84   Hello, doctor.

Doctor Two   Do you recognise me, Angela?

Angela 84   Course I recognise you. Not gonna forget a handsome man like you in a hurry am I?

Doctor Two   Well, thank you, Angela.

Angela 84   You're the nice man from India.

Doctor Two   Almost. Pakistan.

Angela 84   Pakistan. Are you going to take me to Pakistan to meet your family?

Doctor Two   I'll have to ask my wife about that.

Angela 84   A wife. You got kiddies?

Doctor Two   Not yet.

Angela 84   You don't want to leave it too long. I left it too long. There was a girl but we're not in touch any more.

Doctor Three (*approaching*)   Good morning.

Angela 84   Who's he?

Doctor Two   This is my colleague. Doctor Carter.

Angela 84   He's not much of a looker is he? None of the old ladies are gonna want him with the curtain pulled round the bed.

Doctor Two   Doctor Carter's with our mental health team.

Angela 84   Is that right?

Doctor Three   I understand that you've been quite aggressive, Mrs Ravenhill.

Angela 84   That's not true.

Doctor Three   Physically aggressive and also verbally aggressive towards the medical team.

Angela 84   Who told you that? Did Ted tell you that?

Doctor Three   You scalded Mr Ravenhill with a cup of boiling water.

Angela 84   You don't want to believe a word he says.

Doctor Three   A nurse witnessed the incident. She was very concerned for you both.

Angela 84   I'd remember if it happened.

Doctor Three   This ward is not able to cope with aggressive behaviour.

Angela 84   Are you going to send me home?

Doctor Two   Not yet, Angela.

Angela 84   I don't want to go home. I want to go with you to India.

Doctor Two   Doctor Carter's team are going to manage your care for a while.

Angela 84   I want to stay with you. I'll be good as gold.

Doctor Three   Mrs Ravenhill, having consulted with the team here, we are sectioning you under Section 2 of the Mental Health Act.

Angela 84   Mental health?

Doctor Three   You will be moved today to a locked ward more suited to patients displaying aggressive behaviour.

Angela 84   Is it a mental hospital?

Doctor Three   Section 2 allows us to place you in the locked ward for up to twenty-eight days –

Angela 84   I'm not doing that!

Doctor Three   But if you respond well to treatment we will be able to release you before that date.

Angela 84   Did Ted put you up to this?

We hear a **Porter** *arriving.*

Doctor Two   Here's your porter, Angela. They'll take you over to the secure unit.

Angela 84   No thank you very much.

Doctor Two   You'll be safer there.

Angela 84   Will I?

Doctor Two   Oh yes it really is a very nice place. You'll have your own room with a view of the Downs.

Angela 84   Will you come and visit me there?

Doctor Two   I have to stay with the other ladies on this ward.

Angela 84   Watch yourself they're all after you them old ladies.

Doctor Two   I'll do my best to take care. Doctor Carter's team will be able to look after you much better.

Ted 84 (*approaching*)   Hello, Angie.

Angela 84   You're wasting your time, Ted. They're moving me.

Ted 84   Yes I know. They told me.

Angela 84   What you done to your face?

Ted 84   I burnt myself but it's getting better. The doctors explained to me that you're going somewhere safe.

Angela 84   Safe from you.

Ted 84   Don't be like that, Angie. I'll tell Mark they've moved you. So he comes to the new ward on Saturday.

Angela 84   They're on to you. Aren't you, doctor? I don't know anyone called Mark.

Thirty

Suburban garden. **Julie** *draws on her cigarette.*

Angela 30   What was the food like in Spain?

Julie 28   I didn't like it. I mean I ate it but foreign's not the same is it? Where are the boys?

Angela 84 (*internal*)   I've stolen them. Hidden them away. You're not having them.

Angela 30   Ted's taken them up the park. They'll be back soon.

Julie 28   I hope they're not giving Ted any trouble.

Angela 30   Oh no. Ted loves playing with them. He's a big kid himself really.

Julie 28   He wants a boy of his own.

Angela 30   Maybe. He's never mentioned it.

Julie 28   I thought a girl would be nice but then I got my two little horrors. What do you want Angie?

Angela 30   I don't know. I'm not bothered.

Julie 28   Do you think about it?

Angela 30   Not any more.

Julie 28   You said when we were kids that you were going to have seven. Like Snow White and her dwarves.

Angela 30   Did I? I don't remember that.

Julie 28   And Mum said you'd have to live in a shoe.

Angela 30   Now I think . . . if I had none . . . then I suppose . . .

Julie 28   You wouldn't mind?

Angela 30   I don't know.

Boys (*distant*)   Mummy! Mummy!

Angela 30   Here they are. (*Calls.*) Ted! We're in the garden!

Angela 84 (*internal*)   And I was so angry with Julie. For having those two little boys and going off to Spain without them and for blowing her cigarette smoke all over them. But I didn't say anything because I knew it was all wrong me being angry.

Julie 28   Time to go, boys.

Angela 30   You've been very good boys haven't they, Ted?

Ted 30   Oh yes very good.

Angela 30   You gonna let me give you a cuddle goodbye? That's it. Big cuddle goodbye for your Auntie Angela.

Trundle of wheels down a hospital corridor alongside the suburban garden.

Angela 84 (*internal*)   Jemima's sister-in-law, she was happy to have someone else hatch her eggs but Jemima wanted to hatch her eggs all by herself.

The garden fades. A button is pressed. A dialling tone.

Nurse Three (*intercom*)   Hello?

Porter   New patient for you.

Nurse Three (*intercom*)   Come through.

A pair of doors open automatically. The **Porter** *wheels* **Angela 84** *through the doors.*

Nurse Three   Hello. We've been expecting you. Welcome to Downview. You must be Rita.

Angela 84   Am I?

Nurse Three   Mrs Rita Ravenhill.

Angela 84   I don't remember.

Nurse Three   Yes that's you, Rita.

Angela 84   I don't know. Don't bully me.

Nurse Three   Let's have a look at your wristband my love. If you can show me –

Angela 84   No.

Nurse Three   I'm just going to take a little peek – nothing to worry about my love. There we are. Says here – you're Rita.

Angela 84 (*internal*)   Is that who I am? Rita. There was another name only I don't. What's the other name? I want to know my other name.

Nurse Three   We've got a lovely room for you, Rita. All to yourself.

Thirty-One

Suburban kitchen. **Ted 34** *and* **Angela 34** *eating spaghetti Bolognese.*

Ted 34   I finished editing the Jemima film.

Angela 34   Did it turn out alright?

Ted 34   A bit over-exposed in some bits but on the whole not bad.

Angela 34   That's good. When you going to show it us?

Ted 34   I could set up the projector tomorrow night.

Angela 34   Could do. Or . . . does Mark know you finished it?

Ted 34   No. Fast asleep.

Angela 34   Don't tell him it's done. Not just yet. You know what he's like. If he knows it's done there'll be no peace until he's seen it.

Ted 34   Ha! Yes.

Angela 34   Let's save it for his birthday party.

Ted 34   That's a good idea.

Angela 34   He likes it when he's got an audience.

Ted 34   Funny kid.

Angela 34   Ted! Don't say that! Your own son. Honestly!

Ted 34   What does he want for his birthday? Has he told you?

Angela 34   He saw a book up Woolies that he wants.

Ted 34   What's that then?

Angela 34   Little paperback. Only costs a shilling. I said: you can have a bigger present than that, Mark. But no. That's what he wants.

Ted 34   What is it?

Angela 34   How To. It's a series. Mark wants How To Be a Ballet Dancer.

Ted 34   Yeah?

Angela 34   There's pictures. So you can learn all the ballet steps.

Ted 34   Is that what he wants to be? Ballet dancer?

Thirty-Two

Ballet studio. A group of about ten women talking, waiting for the class to start.

Mark 52 *comes through the door.*

Mark 52   Hello. I'm here for the ballet class.

Instantly, the women fall totally silent.

Is there somewhere I can change?

Silence.

I suppose there must be somewhere to change?

Silence.

I bought a jock strap and ballet shoes. It said in the course details to –

Silence.

Or do we just change in here?

Older Woman   No you don't just change in here.

Mark 52   Right. Where do I –?

Older Woman   The changing room next door's for women.

Mark 52   I see yes but I suppose there must be one for men.

Older Woman   We've never had a man before.

Mark 52   I see yes.

Older Woman   So none of us know if there's a man's changing room do we?

Mutter of agreement from the other women.

Mark 52   Right.

He shuffles uncomfortably as the women return to talking. Over this we hear:

Ted 34   I don't want him to be a ballet dancer.

Angela 34   Why not?

Ted 34   I don't know I just don't want my son to be a ballet dancer.

Angela 34   But if he wants the book.

Ted 34   Can't we get him some more Meccano?

Angela 34   He hasn't touched the last lot.

Ted 34   No?

Angela 34   Not once. He made the box into a toy theatre.

Ted 34   If my son is . . . if he's . . .

Angela 34   What?

Ted 34   I don't want him to grow up funny. He'll be lonely. Unpopular.

Angela 34   It's just a phase. They have phases. When I was his age I wanted to be in films. I wanted to be like Deanna Durbin and sing in all my films.

Ted 34   Really?

Angela 34   And now I'm a housewife. That's the way life is. When you were little

Ted 34   Yes?

Angela 34   what did you want to be?

Ted 34   Normal.

Angela 34   He'll grow out of it. I gave up the Players once we were married didn't I? He won't be doing ballet when he's grown up.

*The door to the ballet studio opens and the **Teacher** enters.*

Teacher   Good morning, everyone!

The women variously say hello and then talk to each other.

Mark 52   Excuse me. I was wondering –

Teacher   Ah you must be (*reads from list*) Mark Ravenhill.

Mark 52   That's right yes.

Teacher   Lovely to see a man on the list.

Mark 52   Yes?

Teacher   We don't have enough men.

Mark 52   Is there a changing room?

Teacher   For the men? I think there's one on the next floor up.

Mark 52   Right. Thanks.

Teacher   We'll wait for you while – have you taken ballet class before?

Mark 52   No never.

Teacher   Well, you'll soon catch up.

Mark 52   I've thought about it but now I decided.

Teacher   Good for you.

Mark 52   Better late than never.

Thirty-Three

Day room in the secure unit. A TV with low sound level plays daytime TV. Several old ladies sitting about.

Nurse Three (*entering*)   In you come, Rita. That's it. This is the Downview day room. Say hello to Rita, ladies.

Several old ladies mutter hello.

Angela 84   Hello. Pleased to meet you.

Nurse Three   Is this chair free for Rita? Yes? Ivy normally takes this chair don't you, my love?

Ivy (*some distance*)   I'm watching the television.

Nurse Three   That's alright, my love. You carry on watching the telly.

Nurse Three   Looks like it's free Rita. Better grab it while we can, my love. Shall I give you a hand, Rita?

Ivy   When's my mummy coming?

Nurse Three   What's that Ivy, my love?

Ivy   When's my mummy coming?

Nurse Three   Not today, my love.

Ivy   Will Mummy come soon?

Nurse Three   I'm not sure, my love.

Ivy   Thank you, Auntie Jean.

Nurse Three (*to* **Angela**) Oh dear. Now she thinks I'm her Auntie Jean. I wonder who she thinks you are, Rita?

Angela 84 (*internal*)   She keeps on saying Rita but I'm sure that's not right.

Nurse Three   That's it, Rita. Are you comfy there?

Angela 84   It's alright. (*Internal.*) If it's not Rita what is it?

Nurse Three   Is it nice being in here after all week in your room, Rita? Doctor Carter said because you've taken your tablets and you're much calmer now I'm allowed to bring you into the day room.

Angela 84   Have you got walnut cake?

Nurse Three   Ooooh, I wish we had, my love. I'd eat it all myself.

Angela 84   You want to watch your figure. Big girl like you.

Nurse Three (*laughs*)   My husband likes a roly poly and I like a spotted dick.

Angela 84   I want walnut cake.

Nurse Three   We've got biscuits. Shall I get you biscuits, Rita?

Angela 84   If you like.

Nurse Three   I'll be back in a minute, Rita.

Angela 84   I'm not called Rita.

Nurse Three   No, my love? What are you called?

Angela 84   I want to be Deanna.

Nurse Three   Is that Irish?

Angela 84   Only it's not Deanna. It's . . . why don't I know?

Nurse Three (*retreating*)   You have a think, my love, while I get the biscuits.

Angela 84 (*internal*)   I was in the kitchen. Peeling potatoes.

Mum   Well, if you don't want to be Rita what do you want to be?

Angela 84 (*internal*)   What did I say?

Angela 15   I want to be Peg o' My Heart.

Angela 84 (*internal*)   No! That's not it. What?

Ivy (*other side of the room*)   Mummy!

Angela 84 (internal) What's she –? Old lady. She's talking to me. What's she saying?

Ivy   Mummy!

Angela 84 (*internal*)   She's calling me Mummy. Am I her mummy?

Ivy (*approaching*)   Why didn't they tell me you were coming to see me, Mummy?

Angela 84   Well. (*Internal.*) I'm not her mummy.

Ivy   I knew you'd come back, Mummy. I don't want to watch the television any more. Can I sit beside you, Mummy?

Angela 84 (*internal*)   She must be mad. She could get nasty. Better . . . (*To* **Ivy**.) If you like.

Ivy (*approaches*)   Did you miss me, Mummy?

Angela 84   Well, I suppose I must have done. (*Internal.*) Must be ninety. I'm younger than her. How can she think I'm her mummy?

Ivy   What was Australia like, Mummy?

Angela 84 (*internal*)   Humour her. (*To* **Ivy**.) Australia? Well . . . it was hot. (*Internal.*) Mad old lady.

Ivy   I'm glad you came back. I want to go to the caravan. I want to go to Bognor and I want to have fish and chips and I want you to read me my story.

Angela 84   Let's see.

Ivy   Please, Mummy.

Angela 84 (*internal*)   I don't know this room. I'm in a strange place. And this mad old lady has – oh! She's putting her arms around me.

Ivy   I love you, Mummy.

Angela 84 (*internal*)   I've got a girl only mine's a little thing. She spoke to me recently and she's coming over with walnut cake. They're murdering kiddies everywhere. I don't want to hurt this one. I want this mad old lady to be happy. Thinks I'm her mummy, I'll play the part. I like acting. (*To*

Ivy.) Alright, darlin', let's go down the caravan and I'll read you *Wind in the Willows*.

Ivy (*tearful*)   Oh, Mummy.

Ivy *sobs*.

Angela 84   There, there, don't upset yourself, darlin'. Mummy's here now. (*Sings softly.*)

The farmer in the dell

The farmer in the dell

Hi-ho, the derry-o

The farmer in the dell

The farmer takes a wife

The farmer takes a wife

Hi-ho, the derry-o

The farmer takes a wife

The wife takes the child

The wife takes the child

Hi-ho, the derry-o

The wife takes the child

Nurse Three (*approaching*)   Is that you singing, Rita?

Angela 84   It's not Rita. It's Angela.

Nurse Three   Is that what you'd like me to call you? Angela?

Angela 84   It's my name.

Nurse Three   You've got a lovely singing voice, Angela.

Angela 84   You think so?

Nurse Three   You could be on the stage. Ivy likes your voice don't you, Ivy?

Ivy   Yes Mummy has a lovely voice.

Angela 84   She thinks I'm her mummy.

Nurse Three (*laughs*)   Oh, Ivy. What we going to do with you? (*To* **Angela**.) I got you some chocolate Bourbons and some rich tea. Is that alright?

Angela 84   Lovely.

Nurse Three   And look you've got a visitor and he's brought you flowers.

Ted 84 (*approaching*)   Hello, Angie, these are for you from the garden.

Angela 84   GET HIM AWAY! AGGGGGHHHH! OUT! OUT! HE'S GONNA KILL ME! HELP!

Ivy   MUMMY! MUMMY! LEAVE MY MUMMY ALONE!

Nurse Three   Rita! Angela! Ivy! Stop it!

Ted 84   Don't you recognise me, Angie? It's Ted. Your husband.

Angela 84   AGGGGHHHHHHHH!

Nurse Three   I'm sorry, Mr Ravenhill, I think maybe today –

Ivy   DON'T HURT MY MUMMY!

Ted 84   Yes I'll leave the flowers in the – (*Retreats.*) I'll come back when she's a bit more – yes.

Angela 84 (*sobbing*)   I don't want to see him I don't want to see him I don't want to see him.

Thirty-Four

Single room in the secure unit. **Angela 84** *is sleeping.*

Mark 52   Angela?

Angela 84   Mmmmm?

Mark 52   Do you recognise me, Angela?

Angela 84   What day is it?

Mark 52   It's Saturday.

Angela 84   Have you come to take me on a cruise?

Mark 52   Not today.

Angela 84   I'm waiting for a handsome man to come to take me away on a cruise.

Mark 52   I said I'd come down today. I'm your son.

Angela 84   Are you?

Mark 52   Do you remember that you've got a son?

Angela 84 (*internal*)   So many people looking for a mum and they all come to me.

There's a girl. I had a girl. Not the old lady in there. My own girl. My daughter.

Mark 52   You did have a girl before me, Mum, yes.

Angela 84   I want to see her.

Mark 52   But she died.

Angela 84   Oh. Did they kill her?

Mark 52   No she was a miscarriage.

Angela 84   Did I go to the funeral?

Mark 52   They didn't have funerals for miscarried babies then. Would you have liked her to have a funeral?

Angela 84   Oh yes I would very much. She wasn't killed?

Mark 52   No, Mum.

Angela 84   They killed my sister.

Mark 52   Who killed your sister?

Angela 84   I don't know their names.

Mark 52   Do you mean your sister Julie?

Angela 84   That's right yes they killed my sister Julie.

Mark 52   They didn't kill Julie, Mum. She died of cancer.

Angela 84   Did she?

Mark 52   We went to her funeral last year and you saw her boys all grown-up. Do you remember that?

Angela 84   No.

Mark 52   You wore a new blouse.

Angela 84   Did I look smart?

Mark 52   You did.

Angela 84   Will you brush my hair? I don't like them seeing me all scruffy.

Mark 52   If there's a brush then I'll –

He searches in bedside drawer.

Ah! Here we are. You sit up and I'll – let's get you smart.

He brushes her hair.

Mark 52   Was Julie your favourite sister?

Angela 84   I don't have favourites. I suppose she was.

Thirty-Five

Suburban living room. Birthday party guests including **Ted 34,** **Angela 34** *and* **Julie 32** *are singing.*

Guests (*all together*)   Happy birthday, Mark!

Ted 34   Hip hip!

All   Hooray!

Chatter.

Mark 4 (*close*)   Mummy can we show the film now?

Angela 34   I don't see why not. Ted you got everything set up to show the film?

Ted 34   All ready.

Angela 34   Alright then. Excuse me, everyone! Hello!

Chatter.

Mark's made a special film that he wants to show you all. Go on, Mark, tell them what it's about.

Mark 4   This is the story of a duck that went to the woods and laid her eggs and then she did a dance around her eggs.

Angela 34   Where should we sit, Ted?

Ted 34   You all need to be sort of in the middle and looking at that wall.

Excited chatter and moving of furniture as everyone gets themselves into place.

Angela 34   Already, everyone? Good. Switch it on, Ted. The Tale of Jemima the duck.

A clunky old projector whirrs and clicks as the film begins and the guests whoop and clap during:

Angela 84 (*internal*)   Jemima was all in tears.

The dogs had killed the Fox but they'd eaten her eggs too.

It wasn't safe out in the world.

Jemima – you'll have to go back to the farm.

We cross-fade back into the room in the secure ward.

Mark 52   Ted wants to see you.

Angela 84   I don't want to see him. Not after what he's done.

Mark 52   What's he done, Mum?

Angela 84   You know.

Mark 52   No I don't know. That's why I'm asking you. What's he done?

Angela 84   They take the children. It's so horrible. They capture the children and then they take them in the houses and under the stairs and then they're under the street. I can hear them calling out from under the street because they're so frightened only I can't get to them to save them.

Mark 52   Who's taking the children?

Angela 84   Ted and the neighbours and the police and the doctor. All the children screaming from under the street and now they're murdering them every day killing more and more kiddies. I can't stand it! I can't stand it! They got to stop it or I'll go mad. I can't go on living like this!

She sobs.

What am I going to do?

The chugging of the cine-projector leads us back into the suburban living room.

Mark 4   And that's the end of the film.

The guests cheer and clap.

Julie 32   Well done, Mark, that was lovely. That was lovely, Angie.

Angela 34   Say thank you, Auntie Julie.

Mark 4   Thank you, Auntie Julie.

Julie 32   Is that what you want to be then, Mark, is it? A dancer?

Angela 34   Do you want to have a smoke, Julie, in the garden?

Julie 32   Do you want to be a ballet dancer when you grow up?

Mark 4   Yes I'm going to be a ballet dancer.

Angela 34   Oooh look, Mark, you've got some more presents to open. Over there. Go on.

Julie 32   Angela, you don't think Mark's a bit . . .

Angela 34   A bit what?

Julie 32   Well you know – ballet dancer – it's a bit . . .

Angela 34   A bit what, Julie?

Julie 32   A bit . . .

Angela 34   Yes?

Julie 32   You know.

Angela 34   No I don't.

Julie 32   I mean you want to watch out.

Angela 34   Watch out for what?

Julie 32   That he doesn't grow up to be a great big poof.

Angela 84 (*internal*)   And the anger in me. Like I was the dog and she was the fox.

Growling, barking.

Teeth ripping at the flesh.

Great squeals of pain.

Screaming and biting and tearing and barking and howling and roaring and cracking and crunching.

Mouths all bloody.

Fox fur under my claws.

Jemima knew that they had killed the fox.

But I didn't do that and I looked at Julie and I said:

Angela 34   And what if he is? Go outside and have your cigarette.

My son will grow up to be whatever he wants to be thank you very much. My son can do anything.

Thirty-Six

Room in the secure unit.

Mark 52   Can you see in the mirror?

Angela 84   Yes I can see in the mirror. I'm an old lady, aren't I?

Mark 52   You are, Mum, you're a very old lady. Do you like your hair?

Angela 84   Are you a hairderesser?

Mark 52   No.

Angela 84   Are you my sister?

Mark 52   Would you like me to be your sister?

Angela 84   You can't be my sister can you because you're a man. Are you my son?

Mark 52   That's right.

Angela 84   Are you called Mark?

Mark 52   That's me. Yes. I'm Mark Ravenhill. Ted's outside in the car. Waiting.

Angela 84   I can't see him.

Mark 52   He wants to see you. He loves you.

Angela 84   That's what he says.

Mark 52   I want you to talk to Ted.

Angela 84   I'm frightened.

Mark 52   Angela I think . . . I think we've all got muddled. All of our heads have got confused. Everyone's memories have played tricks and we've all got ourselves upset.

Angela 84   Is that right?

Mark 52   All of us have got confused and then our minds have imagined things and we've got angry with each other. Is that what it feels like to you, Angela?

Angela 84   Yes it does.

Mark 52   And if we forget how upset we've all become and just sit together and have tea and walnut cake then I think we'll all be alright, ok?

Angela 84   Do you think so? (*Internal.*) Is he the Fox? Or is he a goodie? I can't work it out.

Mark 52   So I'm going to text Ted now and say that he can come in and sit with us for a bit, alright?

Angela 84   Mark, am I mad?

Mark 52   We're all a bit mad aren't we?

Angela 84   Oh. I don't want to be mad. That's the most frightening of all.

Mark 52   Shall I send Ted the message?

Angela 84   Yes.

Angela 84 (*internal*)   Jemima went back to the farm and she laid a big batch of eggs but only four of them hatched.

The ping of a text message arriving.

Ted 84 (*approaching*)   Hello, Angela.

Angela 84   Hello, Ted.

Ted 84   This is a nice room isn't it? You can see right over the Downs.

Angela 84 (*internal*)   And Jemima knew that her nerves were too bad and as long as she lived she would never be a good sitter. And she promised herself never to lay another egg ever again.

Ted 84   Angela.

Angela 84   Yes, Ted?

Ted 84   I love you.

He kisses her.

Angela 84   Who do you have to speak to round here to get some walnut cake? . . . And I love you, Ted.

Thirty-Seven

Ballet studio. The class members are talking in groups.

Teacher   All right, ladies and gentleman. Break time is over. Now that we're all nicely hydrated let's get back into our seconde at the barre shall we?

Still talking the group take up their positions.

Teacher (*close*)   Everything alright, Mark?

Mark 52   I just had a text message. In the break. About my mum.

Teacher   Do you need to call back?

Mark 52   No. She died this morning.

Teacher   Oh I'm so sorry. If you need to leave.

Mark 52   No. I'll stay.

Teacher   If you're sure.

Mark 52   I'm sure. I want to carry on.

Ballet music and the sound of the class dancing.

Teacher   That's it, ladies! On we go!

9 781350 255593